THE BLUE BOOK OF DOGS

THE BLUE BOOK OF DOGS

SPORTING · WORKING · HERDING · NON-SPORTING

JULIE MUSZYNSKI

COLLINS | DESIGN

An Imprint of HarperCollinsPublishers

THE BLUE BOOK OF DOGS
SPORTING · WORKING · HERDING · NON-SPORTING

First Edition

First published in 2007 by:
Collins Design
An Imprint of HarperCollins*Publishers*
10 East 53rd Street
New York, NY 10022
Tel: (212) 207-7000
Fax: (212) 207-7654
collinsdesign@harpercollins.com
www.harpercollins.com

Distributed throughout the world by:
HarperCollins*Publishers*
10 East 53rd Street
New York, NY 10022
Fax: (212) 207-7654

Design: Agnieszka Stachowicz

Library of Congress Cataloging-in-Publication Data

Muszynski, Julie.
  The blue book of dogs / Julie Muszynski. -- 1st ed.
      p. cm.
  ISBN-13: 978-0-06-123888-8 (hardcover)
  ISBN-10: 0-06-123888-0 (hardcover)
  1. Dogs. I. Title.

  SF426.M875 2007
  636.7'1--dc22

                                                    2006101740

Printed in China
First Printing, 2007

FOR DAD

I am I because my little dog knows me.

—Gertrude Stein

PREFACE

The Blue Book of Dogs and its partner, *The Red Book of Dogs* were inspired by the original titles written in 1939 by Robert Briggs Logan. Today, nearly three quarters of a century later, they return with the original breed descriptions, updated and enhanced with a fun and interesting facts and additional images.

At dog shows, all breeds are divided into six groups—sporting dogs, hounds, working dogs, herding dogs, terriers, toys, and non-sporting dogs. *The Blue Book of Dogs* describes those breeds in the sporting dogs, working dogs, herding dogs, and non-sporting dogs groups, while *The Red Book of Dogs* includes hounds, terriers, and toy dogs all arranged alphabetically within their groups for quick reference.

The sport of breeding dogs throughout the centuries has resulted in the dog becoming an animal more diversified in appearance and value to man than any other living being. Dogs range in size from the one-pound Chihuahua to the two hundred-pound St. Bernard; from the stubby-legged Dachshund to the huge Irish Wolfhound standing as high as six feet on his hind legs. They may be almost any color, according to their breed.

The story of the dog goes back to the beginning of human history when dog aided man in his daily hunt for food. Through the ages, the dog has remained by the side of humans, helping to fight their battles, to guard their homes, and to serve in numerous other ways.

Today, the dog's service to humankind has narrowed to that for which he is better fitted than any other animal. He gives us, in this busy life, the balance we need through his day-in day-out companionship. No matter how great our worries, a dog's friendship and consistent loyalty never subsides; it soothes our ruffled feelings, eliminates our loneliness, restores our good spirits, and, by actual example in trust, patience, and gratitude, gives us the courage to have continued confidence in humankind.

SPORTING • WORKING • HERDING • NON-SPORTING

AMERICAN WATER SPANIEL
Sporting

Distinctly North American in both origin and utility, the American Water Spaniel is a breed with an excellent hunting ability and a merry disposition combined. He is ideally fitted for hunting in this country.

Just how early breeders originated the American Water Spaniel has never been recorded, though his general appearance definitely suggests the crossing of Irish Water Spaniels, Curly-Coated Retrievers, and the now extinct English Spaniel. Resembling the Irish Water Spaniel except for his smaller proportions and lack of the Irish's topknot, the American sports a closely curled coat that is valuable in water, rough-going, and it may be colored either solid liver or dark chocolate.

The standard weight of the breed is heavier than that of a large Cocker and lighter than that of a Springer Spaniel. Weight specifications are twenty-eight to forty-five pounds for males and twenty-five to forty pounds for females, while the height is between fifteen and eighteen inches at the shoulders.

According to the American Kennel Club, "the American Water Spaniel was the first breed developed in the United States as an all-around hunter that could retrieve from boats."

The American Water Spaniel is Wisconsin's official state dog.

The American Water Spaniel has an excellent sense of smell, which enables him to spring game from the most obscure locations.

The American Water Spaniel was bred to be smaller than other hunting breeds in order to fulfill the need for a dog that could hunt on land and in the marsh, and easily fit into the hunter's canoe.

In 1920, the first American Water Spaniel was registered with the United Kennel Club by Dr. F.J. Preifer, of New London, Wisconsin.

BRITTANY SPANIEL
Sporting

The sporting breed Brittany Spaniel works similarly to the setter in the field. Originally, in France, he was used principally for hunting woodcock, but today he is an excellent all-around sporting dog.

The Brittany Spaniel resembles both a long-legged Springer Spaniel and a setter, being energetic and intelligent in appearance. The wavy hair of the dog lies close to the body and can have only two color combinations, either white and liver or white and orange. He stands from seventeen to twenty inches in height.

The outstanding features of the Brittany Spaniel, in addition to his color allowances, are his tail, which is either absent or but an inch or so in length, and his rather short ears set high on his head.

He is widely admired as a dog capable of many varied uses in the field and often surpasses more popular breeds widely known for their excellent work in hunting.

The Brittany Spaniel was named after the French province where he originated.

Legend has it that the first Brittany Spaniels were developed in a small town called Pontou in the mid-1800s.

This breed is often depicted in tapestries and in French and Dutch paintings dating back to the seventeenth century, especially in the works of Jean-Baptiste Oudry and Jan Steen.

The Brittany Spaniel has won more Dual Championship titles, in both confirmation and field, than any other sporting breed.

In the eighteenth and nineteenth centuries, farmworkers often used their Brittany Spaniels while hunting and stealing game birds from their wealthy employers' land.

CHESAPEAKE BAY RETRIEVER
Sporting

The Chesapeake Bay Retriever is one of the very few recognized breeds of dogs that are distinctly North American in origin. He came into existence at the beginning of the nineteenth century from the probable crossing of a nondescript duck dog and the Newfoundland. The story is that a ship bound for England from Newfoundland was wrecked in Chesapeake Bay. On this boat were two Newfoundland puppies named Sailor and Canton that mated with local duck dogs to originate the Chesapeake Bay Retriever.

This breed is used mostly for retrieving ducks in water. The dense coat is absolutely waterproof, enabling the dog to withstand the coldest water. His color may range from a dull tan to a dark brown.

The Chesapeake Bay Retriever has a bright and happy disposition. However, he selects his own friends and utterly attaches himself to them. He is a very courageous dog, willing to dive into any kind of water in all sorts of weather and swim any distance to retrieve.

The Chesapeake Bay Retriever can be colored brown, sedge, or deadgrass.

In 1964, this breed was named the official state dog of Maryland.

The Chesapeake Bay Retriever has the amazing ability to retrieve between two hundred and three hundred ducks per day.

President Theodore Roosevelt had a Chesapeake Bay Retriever named Sailor Boy.

The Chesapeake Bay Retriever is the mascot of the University of Maryland, Baltimore County.

CLUMBER SPANIEL
Sporting

The Clumber Spaniel is the most massive and the heaviest of the spaniels, weighing as much as sixty-five pounds. His coat is straight and silky in texture, and it is colored lemon or orange with a few white markings, but lemon is the more desirable coloring of the two.

The Clumber, which originated in England partly from the Basset Hound, is a dignified dog. He is slow-moving, but when working at his duties of flushing cock, the dog is thorough and deliberate.

His light-colored coat, short but strong legs, sturdy neck, and noble-appearing head show this dog to be a powerful working member of the spaniel family. He is sedate in his movements but not in the least clumsy.

This breed is a certain finder of game and a splendid retriever when trained for this purpose. He is a good dog for fieldwork and unexcelled when leisurely hunting is desired.

This breed is named after the Duke of Newcastle's home in England, Clumber Park.

Clumber Spaniels originally hunted in packs of eight or ten, but today they hunt alone—silently, with little or no bark, which allows close proximity to the game.

Often referred to as the Dog of Dignity, the Clumber Spaniel is one of the most aristocratic of all spaniels due to the long and noble shape of his body, his quiet and dignified disposition, and his distinctive preference for hunting pheasant.

The Clumber Spaniel was a particular favorite hunting breed of the British royal family. Both Prince Albert and King Edward VII were devoted admirers.

COCKER SPANIEL
AMERICAN VARIETY
Sporting

The smallest breed of all sporting dogs is the Cocker Spaniel. There are two varieties of this merry little dog—the English and the American, which was bred from his older cousin in England. The American Cocker Spaniel weighs from eighteen to twenty-four pounds as compared to the larger English, whose weight can be anywhere from twenty-five to thirty pounds.

Though the American Cocker Spaniel is a sporting dog, he has gained his popularity through owning a splendid disposition; his soulful eyes advertise his gentle nature and willing heart. The Cocker makes a very good pet.

The coat of the Cocker Spaniel, both English and American, is very dense, silky, and sometimes wavy. The Cocker is a rainbow of colors. It is permissible for the breed to be almost any color from pure white to jet black, including parti-colors.

Few breeds are as ready for both work and play as the Cocker.

🐕

Today, the Cocker Spaniel remains one of the most popular and beloved breeds in America.

🐕

Known for her long, flowing ears and large brown eyes, a Cocker Spaniel named Lady was the glamorous, love-struck star of the Disney animated classic *Lady and the Tramp*.

🐕

Katharine Hepburn owned three Cocker Spaniels: Peter, Button, and Mica; Oprah Winfrey owns two named Solomon and Sophie.

🐕

In 1952, Richard Nixon gave his famous Checkers Speech, denying accusations that he had received illegal campaign contributions. In it, he claimed that Checkers, his family's Cocker, was the one contribution he'd received and that "regardless of what they say, we're gonna keep it."

🐕

In the show ring, blond Cockers are referred to as ASCOB—Any Solid Color Other than Black.

COCKER SPANIEL
ENGLISH VARIETY
Sporting

The older phase of the Cocker is the hardier of the two, and it is the dog more frequently used in the field. The name for this breed was derived from his original use of hunting woodcock in England. He is an active, intelligent little hunter and very clever in retrieving on both land and water. The English Cocker, in addition to his retrieving ability, can hold his own with many breeds in flushing game.

The Cocker Spaniel is a descendant of the spaniel family, whose historical records date back to the fourteenth century, and is very closely related to the other spaniels. The English type of Cocker Spaniel is very similar to the Field Spaniel, weight being practically the only distinction, whereas the American Cocker is a breed with his own appearance.

The Cocker Spaniel is a true lover of his home and family and makes a good house dog. He is loyal and can adapt himself readily to the changing moods of his master.

Elizabeth Barrett Browning owned an English Cocker Spaniel named Flush, which inspired her poem *To Flush, My Dog* and later inspired Virginia Woolf to write *Flush: A Biography*, a dog's view of his beloved owner.

Blessings on thee, dog of mine,
Pretty Collars make thee fine,
Sugared milk make fat thee!
Pleasures wag on in thy tail,
Hands of gentle motion fail
Nevermore, to pat thee
—Elizabeth Barrett Browning, from *To Flush, My Dog*

Thanks to his happy disposition and constantly wagging tail, the English Cocker is often referred to as the Merry Cocker.

President John F. Kennedy owned an English Cocker named Shannon.

In Cuban airports, English Cocker Spaniels are trained and used as sniffers, locating drugs in travelers' luggage.

CURLY-COATED RETRIEVER
Sporting

One of the most ancient of the retrieving family of dogs is the Curly-Coated Retriever, which comes from England and Scotland. It is generally believed that the Irish Water Spaniel, and possibly the Poodle, had much to do with his origin.

The outstanding feature of the Curly-Coated Retriever is his coat, which is a mass of short, crisp curls that enable him to dive into the iciest of waters to retrieve ducks and other feathered game. This same coat makes it possible for him to run in the densest of coverts without punishment to his body.

The breed is a strong, intelligent-looking dog and possesses remarkable staying power. He also has a splendid temperament, making him one of the easiest of all gundogs to train.

Curly-Coated Retrievers usually weigh about sixty pounds.

The Curly-Coated Retriever has been in existence since the 1850s and was one of the first breeds classified as a retriever.

"Once [the Curly-Coated Retriever] accepts someone, that person could not wish for a truer or more loyal friend in any situation."
—*Dogs*

This breed is popular in Australia and New Zealand, but is not as well known in the United States.

The Curly-Coated Retriever is the tallest of the retriever breeds.

The Curly-Coated Retriever was first shown at England's Birmingham Show in 1860.

ENGLISH SETTER
Sporting

The English Setter is essentially a sporting gentleman's dog. He is an active, rugged, out-of-doors breed with great scenting ability. He is an ideal field dog for the setting of game.

In addition to his ability as a sporting dog, the English Setter is a good house dog. He possesses a mild, even temperament.

The English Setter probably originated from crosses with the old Spanish Pointer and one or more breeds of the spaniel family.

This dog is beautiful in appearance. His movement is graceful, and his light color, flecked with tan, gray, or orange, adds to this beauty. The coat is rather long and lies flat to the body. The feathering behind the legs and beneath the tail gives the English Setter an aristocratic profile.

The name Setter comes from the "set," or pointing position, that this dog exhibits when he has discovered game.

There are two types of English Setters: the Laverack Setter, named after its breeder, Edward Laverack, and the Llewellin Setter, named after breeder R. Rucell Llewellin.

President Franklin D. Roosevelt owned a Llewelin Setter named Winks, and President Herbert Hoover owned an English Setter named Eaglehurst Gillette.

Count Noble, an English Setter that was the top sporting dog of his day, has been preserved and can be seen today at the National Bird Dog Museum in Grand Junction, Tennessee.

English Setters have been the subjects of paintings by Gustav Muss-Arnolt, Edmund Henry Osthaus, and Percival Leonard Rosseau.

FIELD SPANIEL
Sporting

The Field Spaniel is another member of the spaniel family from England, closely related to the Cocker Spaniel and the Sussex Spaniel and, in fact, originating from a cross between these two breeds, which occurred around the middle of the nineteenth century.

This breed is a solid and handsome dog with a good balance of height (eighteen inches) and weight (forty to fifty pounds). His coat is termed "self-colored"—black or colors away from black, with tan markings over the eyes and on the cheeks, feet, and pasterns. The coat is usually waved slightly, rather dense and of silky texture. He has abundant feathering rather similar to that of the setters.

The general appearance of the Field Spaniel suggests a levelheaded sporting breed built for activity and endurance. He is a good combination of utility and beauty, and possesses great perseverance and agility.

The Field Spaniel has a kindly nature and a friendly disposition.

Developed at a time when dog showing was becoming popular, the Field Spaniel was bred specifically for conformation showing.

This breed is rumored to have arrived in the United States on the *Mayflower*.

Dr. Fred Pfiefer—often called the father of the American Water Spaniel—developed a studbook to keep track of the breed, called *Field Dog Stud Book*.

After World War I, the Field Spaniel breed suffered greatly, as many dogs were killed in battle. Following World War II, when many more Field Spaniels died, the breed became threatened with extinction. Today, the Field Spaniel reportedly has the lowest registration of any of the spaniel breeds.

In 1894, the American Kennel Club registered the first Field Spaniel, Cole Shill Rufus.

FLAT-COATED RETRIEVER
Sporting

The Flat-Coated Retriever is an active, intelligent sporting dog from England. This breed is the result of a cross of the Newfoundland and the Labrador Retriever, which he so closely resembles except for the long, flat coat of fine texture. The coat is colored either black or liver. In addition to the Saint John's Newfoundland and the Labrador, there is also evidence of Gordon Setter, Irish Setter, and possibly Russian Tracker blood in the Flat-Coated Retriever.

This sporting dog is a diligent and capable worker, both in water and on land, being possessed of the ability to mark and retrieve in a manner denoting complete efficiency. He loves the water but, at the same time, is more than willing to do very good work on the uplands.

The Flat-Coated Retriever is a powerful dog, but not in the least cumbersome for his size. The breed usually attains a weight of somewhere between sixty and seventy pounds.

Playful and puppylike, the Flat-Coated Retriever is often called the Peter Pan of Dogs.

After World War I and World War II, this breed, like many others, suffered a dangerous decline due to the number of dogs that were killed in the line of duty.

"The Flat-Coated Retriever is a very handsome dog, intelligent, and strong. It has the most expressive face; it looks up at you very often with an expression of mischief, tolerance, and kindness very difficult to define."
—*Dogs*

While not as popular as other retrievers, this breed has always been a favorite hunting dog in sporting circles.

GERMAN SHORTHAIRED POINTER
Sporting

The German Shorthaired Pointer is an all-purpose dog. He has the characteristics of the Pointer in being able to detect game, but he can also retrieve, trail in the field, and even work in water. The German Shorthaired Pointer has a reputation for being a herder of cattle in Germany and a good killer of vermin, as well as working as a general utility dog.

This breed originated from crosses first between the old Spanish Pointer, the English Foxhound, and the Bloodhound, and later with the Pointer that we know today.

As the name implies, the coat is short, flat, and firm. The only colors allowed are liver or liver and white. The weight of the German Shorthaired Pointer varies from forty-five to seventy pounds; height is from twenty-one to twenty-five inches at the shoulders.

This good all-around gundog is a methodical, thorough, and willing worker. At home, he is a great watchdog and a real companion.

Esteemed German writer and Nobel Prize winner for literature Thomas Mann had a German Shorthaired Pointer named Bashan, which was the inspiration for his story *A Man and His Dog*.

In Germany, both varieties of this breed were used to hunt deer, fox, rabbit, pheasant, partridge, woodcock, and duck.

The German Shorthaired Pointer is also known as the *Deutsch Kurzhaar*.

This breed is commonly referred to as the GSP.

Robert B. Parker's mystery series about a detective named Spenser features three German Shorthaired Pointers, all called Pearl. An image of Pearl can be found on some of Parker's book jackets.

GOLDEN RETRIEVER
Sporting

The Golden Retriever is a beautiful dog, with his flat, wavy coat of rich golden color. Though his development has been in England, he should probably be termed a Russian dog because his ancestors were the old Russian Tracker and the Bloodhound.

In the field, the Golden Retriever is both a good retriever and a good setter, being equally at home on land and in the water, where his water-resistant coat comes in handy. He is a symmetrical, active, and powerful dog with good movement. Few other breeds have as kindly an expression as does the Golden Retriever.

This handsome breed somewhat resembles the Flat-Coated Retriever. He is easily broken to the field and makes a strong, reliable worker. It is interesting to note that this dog breeds absolutely true to his rich golden color.

The ideal weight for the Golden Retriever when in working condition is from sixty-five to seventy-five pounds; the height is twenty to twenty-four inches.

Lord Tweedmouth of Scotland is credited with developing the Golden Retriever.

Golden Retrievers are both excellent hunting dogs and seeing-eye dogs for the blind.

One of the most popular breeds in North America, the Golden Retriever often portrays the quintessential family pet in both television and film. This was the case in *Punky Brewster*, *Full House*, *Air Bud*, and *Fatal Attraction*.

President Gerald Ford owned a Golden Retriever named Liberty, which famously gave birth to a litter of puppies in the White House.

Jimmy Buffet has a Golden Retriever, aptly named Cheeseburger; Oprah Winfrey has three, named Luke, Layla, and Gracie.

GORDON SETTER
Sporting

From Scotland, the Gordon Setter is unusual as a setter, for he is a one-person dog. He is also known as the Black and Tan Setter, his coat being a shiny black with chestnut or mahogany-red markings, similar to those of the Doberman Pinscher, appearing regularly over the body. The breed probably originated along the lines used to perfect other setters, with the addition of a Black and Tan Collie.

The Gordon Setter was developed for work in the hilly countryside of Scotland and is therefore a rather slow worker in comparison with his cousins, the English and the Irish Setters. To offset his slowness, he is a very thorough and painstaking worker with great perseverance. He works best at hunting woodcock and handles that little bird very well.

"In the early 1800s, a Scottish Duke, Alexander Forth of Gordon, often borrowed from farmers of the country some black and red dogs who showed a strange hunting instinct. One female in particular possessed an extraordinary sense of smell and was an infallible pointer. The Duke mated her with his Setters and so began a new breed."

—*The Great Book of Dogs*

Gordon Setters are the heaviest of all three setters.

The Gordon is the only native Scottish gundog and was bred specifically to hunt game birds, especially grouse.

Gordon Setters, like English Setters, were a favorite subject of American artist Gustav Muss-Arnolt.

IRISH SETTER
Sporting

A beautiful mahogany-red coat and a beautiful body make the Irish Setter a strong claimant to the title of most handsome of all breeds. He loves to work in the field and goes about performing his duties of pointing or setting game in a willing and quick manner.

The Irish Setter is very intelligent and trainable. He is happy-go-lucky in nature, though at the same time quite strong willed and bold. He is wonderfully gentle and loyal to his master and makes an excellent companion.

The coat of the Irish Setter is rather long and straight. Feathering, which is a lighter shade of red than that on his body, is present on the back of the fore and hind legs and beneath the tail. He stands about twenty-one to twenty-four inches high.

The heartwarming 1962 Disney film *Big Red* tells the tragic and triumphant adventures of a boy and his stunning Irish Setter, Big Red.

John Steinbeck had an Irish Setter named Toby, which as a puppy chewed up half of the original *Of Mice and Men* manuscript, setting the author back months in his work, as it was the only copy.

In Irish Gaelic, the Irish Setter is called *Madra Rua*, meaning "red dog."

The word "setter" dates back to a time when this breed crouched, or set, in front of a bird as its master put a net over the two animals.

President Richard Nixon owned an Irish Setter named King Timahoe, and President Harry S Truman owned one called Mike.

IRISH WATER SPANIEL
Sporting

It has been said that when all the different breeds of dogs were put together, the Irish Water Spaniel was the last to be given attention. That which was not given to the other breeds was thrown together, and out came the Irish Water Spaniel.

However, this clownish-appearing dog more than makes up for his lack of beauty. He is an excellent water dog able to easily withstand the iciest of waters and retrieve quail and pheasant well.

The Irish Water Spaniel is a very expressive dog. His coat, which sheds water readily, is a cluster of short curls colored a deep, pure liver. This curly coat, together with the topknot on his skull and the ratlike tail, makes him distinctive among dogs. Irish Water Spaniels weigh about forty-five to sixty-five pounds.

Though loyal to his master and family, this breed from Ireland will have little or nothing to do with strangers. He prefers to choose his own friends.

Thanks to its playful and humorous nature, the Irish Water Spaniel is commonly called the clown of the spaniel family.

"She hath more qualities than a Water Spaniel, which is much in a bare Christian."
—William Shakespeare, *Two Gentlemen of Verona*

In the late 1100s, this breed was known as the Shannon Spaniel, Whip Tail Spaniel, and Rat Tail Spaniel.

It is reported that all Irish Water Spaniels can trace their ancestry back to a dog named Boatswain, which was owned by the breed's founder, Justin McCarthy, in the 1800s.

The Irish Water Spaniel is believed to be a descendant of either the Curly-Coated Retriever and the Poodle or the Irish Setter and the Poodle.

LABRADOR RETRIEVER

Sporting

The Labrador Retriever from Newfoundland is valued for his marvelous ability to swim and retrieve in water. He is an exceptional gundog for ducks and geese, the work being great sport for him. He is also an outstanding breed for work in the field.

In comparison with the other retrievers, the Labrador is powerfully built. His coat is distinctive in that it is hard and quite short. Black is the most common color, although there are some specimens in other whole colors of yellow, brown, and liver.

The Labrador is similar to a small Newfoundland. He has an ideal disposition, and his natural cleanliness makes him a good dog for the home when he is not out hunting with his master.

The breed stands twenty-two to twenty-five inches high at the shoulder.

The Labrador Retriever is one of the most popular breeds in the United States.

Two heroic Labs were present during the World Trade Center attacks on September 11, 2001. Roselle, a guide dog, led her owner down more than seventy flights of smoke-filled stairs. Sirus, a police dog, was the only canine that lost his life in the attacks; 250 police officers attended a memorial service in his honor.

The children's book classic *Old Yeller* depicts a relationship between a young boy and a yellow Labrador Retriever. Disney later adapted the book as a feature film starring a Lab named Spike.

President Bill Clinton had a chocolate Labrador Retriever, which he named after his beloved Uncle Buddy. Today, the former president owns another chocolate Labrador, Seamus.

POINTER
Sporting

The Pointer received his name from the manner in which he locates the presence of birds—by standing stiffly toward the hidden bird with tail out behind him and head extended.

It is probable that the Pointer is the result of a cross between the ancient Spanish Pointer and the Southern Hound of England. He owes his development to English fanciers. The Pointer's coat is short, flat, and firm, colored liver and white, either spotted or ticked. He weighs between forty-five and seventy-five pounds and stands between twenty-three and twenty-eight inches high.

The Pointer is a specialist at finding birds. Thanks to his remarkable sense of smell, he can distinguish a bird and "point" it out to the hunter while running at full speed. Compared to his relative the setter, this great bird dog is not affectionate. He is not quick to make friends, but once his friendship is obtained, it is lasting.

The dog chosen for the Westminster Kennel Club logo was a Pointer named Sensation. Since 1936, an embossed image of this prestigious pooch has been the cover of the catalog for the annual Westminster Kennel Club All Breed Dog Show, held at New York City's Madison Square Garden.

American artists Gustav Muss-Arnolt, Edmund Henry Osthaus, and Percival Leonard Rosseau often featured Pointers in their paintings.

The Pointer's hunting instinct develops when he is two months old.

A Pointer named Judy, the only animal officially registered as a Japanese prisoner of war, was awarded the Dickin Medal in 1946. The citation reads: "For magnificent courage and endurance in Japanese prison camps, which helped maintain morale among her fellow prisoners and also for saving lives through her intelligence and watchfulness."

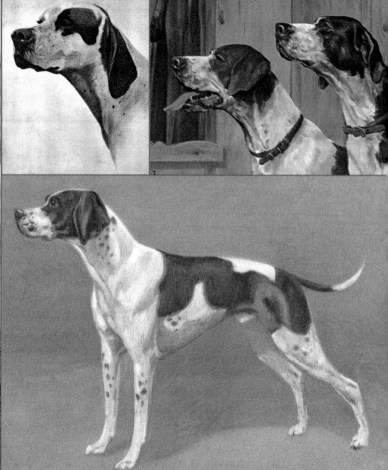

SPRINGER SPANIEL

ENGLISH VARIETY

Sporting

The English Springer Spaniel is hailed as a real springer of game. Under modern sporting conditions, the Springer is a fine all-around gundog for both furred and feathered game. Like other spaniels, the Springer does not point the game for the hunter but runs in and flushes it into the air for the shoot. In addition to this method of work, the Springer is a great retriever in water.

The English Springer Spaniel is an enthusiastic worker. He loves the sport of hunting and is always obedient, always jovial. His coat is of medium length, lying close to his body, and it may be any color but red and white or lemon and white. He stands between nineteen and twenty inches at the shoulders and weighs between forty-nine and fifty-five pounds.

This ideal hunting breed is a perfect combination of utility and beauty; his attractive pacing stride displays a dog that possesses both speed and endurance.

The Springer has been around for so long that he's considered the founder of all hunting spaniels.

In 1297, an English Springer Spaniel named Merlin MacDonald aided the Scottish hero Sir William Wallace in the defeat of the English army at the Battle of Stirling Bridge.

Millie—one of President George H.W. Bush's three Springer Spaniels—was the only White House dog to have her own *New York Times* best seller, *Millie's Book*, which reportedly outsold the president's own memoir. Millie also appeared on the cover of *Life* magazine.

An English Springer Spaniel named Ch. Chinoe's Admant James won Best in Show at the Westminster Kennel Club All Breed Dog Show in 1971 and 1972.

In 2007, Ch. Felicity's Diamond Jim, also known as James, was awarded the Best in Show trophy.

SPRINGER SPANIEL

WELSH VARIETY

Sporting

The outstanding feature of this breed is that he can be only one combination of colors—red and white—though it can be said that the Welsh Springer Spaniel is also noted for his ability to withstand extreme temperatures, either hot or cold.

His desire to please his master in the field matches that quality of his cousin the English Springer. The Welsh is a hunter of great endurance and is capable of working long hours over the roughest ground. He is both a water and a land retriever, and is an excellent flusher of game.

In size, the Welsh Springer Spaniel can be classified as a dog heavier than the Cocker Spaniel but lighter than the English Springer—he weighs thirty-five to forty pounds.

The Welsh Springer Spaniel, known in Wales as a Starter, is a great companion for both the lone hunter and the child, being a merry dog but of gentle nature. He is a pal in every sense of the word.

The Welsh Springer Spaniel dates back to 7000 B.C., and he was formerly called the Welsh Cocker Spaniel.

When he discovers game, the Welsh Springer Spaniel's tail wags faster.

"The Welsh Springer and the English Springer are entirely different breeds and do not represent 'varieties of a Springer Spaniel.'"
—The American Kennel Club

SUSSEX SPANIEL
Sporting

The name of this breed is derived from the place of his origin—Sussex, England. He is often termed the Golden Spaniel, as the one and only color found in this breed is a rich golden liver.

The Sussex Spaniel is built low to the ground and is, therefore, rather slow in fieldwork. This does not prevent him from being a good sporting dog. He is a thorough upland hunter, sometimes giving tongue on scent.

The Sussex Spaniel runs close to the size of the Springer Spaniel. The weight of the dog varies from thirty-five to forty-five pounds, the heavier weight being most common.

The personality of the Sussex Spaniel is that of a cheerful dog that loves work. He is an attractive dog, with his abundant, richly colored coat, slightly waved or lying flat to his body. His beautiful, free gait and graceful tail carriage add much to this attractiveness.

"There is no other animal, which has his coloring except the lion…the Sussex also have the same big bones and big feet, and something of the same steady way of regarding you that the lion does."
—Joy Freer, breeder

The Sussex is one of the oldest and rarest of the Spaniel breeds.

Sussex Spaniels can be seen in the paintings of English artists Maud Earl and Arthur Wardle.

This breed, like so many others, faced extinction after so many dogs died during World War II.

"On the trail he barks continuously like the Bloodhound, and runs with a casual gait that is different from that of all other Spaniels."
—*The Great Book of Dogs*

WIREHAIRED POINTING GRIFFON
Sporting

This dog, known almost as widely as the Rough-Coated German Pointer, is outstanding as a hunting breed. He has a fine nose, is a real retriever, loves to work in water, and, above all, possesses the courage and ability to fight dangerous wounded game. He is a good worker in either cover or open.

The Wirehaired Pointing Griffon is a Dutch breed. He is somewhat slow in working but very deliberate. The coat appears to be unkempt, being very hard, stiff, and dry, and colored a steel gray or gray white with chestnut splashes. The height may be from twenty to twenty-four inches.

The Wirehaired Pointing Griffon is an unexcelled pointer in addition to retrieving both furred and feathered game. He goes in the water in any weather, his coat giving him thorough protection.

Seventy-five to 150 Wirehaired Pointing Griffon puppies are bred in the United States each year, making this breed extremely rare.

This breed has the longest name of all hunting dogs.

The Wirehaired Pointing Griffon was developed by E. K. Korthals in the late 1800s and is believed to be the result of mixing Barbets, French and German Pointers, German Griffons, Spaniels, and a Setter.

The Pointing Griffon is known as the Korthals Griffon in many regions of the world.

The first Wirehaired Pointing Griffon ever registered with the American Kennel Club was named Zolette.

ALASKAN MALAMUTE
Working

The Alaskan Malamute is one of the three recognized Arctic sled dogs, the others being the Eskimo and the Siberian Husky. The Malamute is one of the most capable sled pullers and a native of Alaska.

Malamutes can be various colors but are mostly black and white or a wolfish gray. Their coat is typical of one that can withstand the rigors of the frozen North. There is an undercoat of woolly fur and a rather coarse outercoat that stands straight out from the body. Around the neck is a thick coat of furry texture much longer than the fur on the rest of the body.

This northern dog is large, weighing as much as eighty pounds, and with a strong, somewhat compact physique.

The outstanding feature of the Malamute is probably his face, which is marked with a mask, causing his wolflike eyes to stand out. Malamutes are dogs of endurance and are capable of pulling sleds over the frozen northland prairies for days at a time.

The Alaskan Malamute is named after the Western Alaskan Mahlemut tribe. When their parents went out to hunt, children were watched over by the breed.

George Lucas's Alaskan Malamute, Indiana, was thought to be the inspiration for the *Star Wars* character, Chewbacca.

The Alaskan Malamute is one of the oldest of the Arctic sled dog breeds.

Unlike most breeds, the Alaskan Malamute—along with the Siberian Husky—howls instead of barks.

These dogs have participated in countless polar expeditions and are known for their incredible navigational sense in blizzards.

Alaskan Malamutes have been used for hunting moose, polar bears, and wolves.

BERNESE MOUNTAIN DOG
Working

Mountainous Switzerland claims this well-balanced dog, which is similar to the St. Bernard but smaller. For his size, this breed makes a fine pet for the home. His height runs from twenty-one to twenty-seven inches.

The coat of the Bernese Mountain Dog is long, soft, and quite silky in texture for a breed capable of withstanding rigorous weather. The colors are always black and tan with white markings.

This breed is the only one of four Swiss mountain dogs recognized as a pure breed in North America; others from this country the Large Swiss Mountain Dog, the Appenzell, and the Entlebuch.

The Bernese Mountain Dog is racy in build, active, and alert. He can best be described as a dog of thoroughness and capable of performing a great many varied deeds that are useful to humans. Of course, that work for which he is most noted is as a puller of milk carts. He is used especially in the Swiss canton of Berne.

This breed is also known as the *Berner Sennenhunde* and the *Bouvier Bernois*; it was named after the canton of Berne in Switzerland.

More than two thousand years ago, ancestors of the Bernese Mountain Dog arrived in Switzerland with invading Roman soldiers. The Romans used this breed for fighting, equipping the dogs with large, leather, studded collars.

In 1996, a Bernese Mountain Dog named Ernest ran for the United States Congress, failing to win the seat because the Federal Election Commission revoked his candidacy after learning that Ernest was not human.

Bernese Mountain Dogs are excellent farm dogs, as they can drive cattle and watch over the land. They are also wonderful companions.

There were very few Bernese Mountain Dogs before World War I, but in 1892, the Swiss financier Franz Schertenleib revived the breed, resulting in a much larger population.

BOXER
Working

The Boxer is a stocky dog of medium size and short coat, usually fawn. His alertness and courage make him a marvelous protector of the home. The breed is rather distrustful of strangers, friendly but fierce when aroused.

This dog has in the past been put to use in a great many ways. First of all, he is a peerless guard dog. In Germany, he has for years been a valuable addition to the police force, and many are regular members of the German army. Though the breed name suggests an English dog, he is strictly German in origin.

The Boxer is a proud, sedate-looking dog. He holds his head high and always stands with the erectness of the Great Dane. When he moves, it is with vigor and stateliness.

The distinguishing feature of the Boxer is his well-proportioned head, short muzzle, and powerful body. He is from ten to twenty-four inches high.

According to the American Kennel Club, Boxers are the seventh most popular breed in the United States.

While playing or fighting, the Boxer spars with his front paws much like a prizefighter, which is a trait unique to this breed.

"There is a delightful fable, which says that when God was modeling all the different breeds of dogs, he finally came to the Boxer 'and this dog,' he said 'will be the most beautiful of all the dogs of the world.' On hearing these words, the Boxer could not wait to see his image; before the clay was dry, he ran headlong into the nearest mirror and his nose was squashed flat." —*Dogs*

The Boxer was originally bred for bullbaiting and dogfighting until these sports were outlawed, causing the breed to greatly diminish in numbers.

BULLMASTIFF
Working

The name of this dog reflects those breeds used to originate him—the Bulldog and the Mastiff.

The Bullmastiff is typically a guard dog. He does not bark and raise a commotion when spying a stranger entering the gate of his master's home. He merely walks down in his somber way, meets the stranger, and then accompanies him to the doorway, never taking his eyes away until his master permits the stranger to enter his home. And woe be to the party whom the master does not welcome.

The general appearance of the Bullmastiff is that of a tremendously powerful dog, yet he is symmetrical and agile. This breed, which has great endurance for its size, varies from twenty-four to twenty-seven inches in height and weighs about one hundred pounds.

It has been proved in many instances that this superlative guardian has a nose almost as accurate for trailing as the tracking Bloodhound.

The Bullmastiff was known as the gamekeeper's night dog because of his ability to guard large estates in England from armed poachers.

In the movie *Turner and Hooch*, Tom Hanks starred as a detective named Turner; an unruly Bullmastiff played his sidekick, Hooch.

In *Rocky*, Rocky's Bullmastiff, Butkus, was played by the real-life pet of the film's star, Sylvester Stallone.

Between 1928 and 1940, diamond manufacturer and retailer De Beers used Bullmastiffs as guard dogs at their diamond mines in South Africa.

DOBERMAN PINSCHER
Working

The noble Doberman Pinscher, classed as a working dog but more similar to a terrier in his traits, is one of the most useful of all breeds. He is easily trained. During World War I, he became famous as a hardy breed capable of carrying messages over the most treacherous battlefields. Since that period, the Doberman, along with the German Shepherd Dog, has been used extensively in police work and also as a seeing-eye dog for the blind.

The Doberman originated in Germany in the latter part of the nineteenth century, probably from the German Shepherd Dog, the Rottweiler, and, principally, the Manchester Terrier.

This graceful and fearless dog stands from twenty-four to twenty-eight inches high. The coat is short and close, colored black, brown, or blue and always with sharply defined red-rust markings regularly appearing on the head and legs.

Herr Louis Dobermann, a prominent tax collector and part-time breeder, developed the Doberman Pinscher breed in order to have a dog that could protect him from thieves he encountered on his tax-collecting journeys.

"It is said there is no such thing as a bad Doberman, only a bad owner."
—*The Great Book of Dogs*

Always Faithful, a life-size bronze statue of a real-life Doberman, is located at the War Dog Cemetery on the grounds of the U.S. Naval Base in Guam.

Nicknamed the Dobe, this breed originated in Apolda, Germany, around 1890.

The Doberman is often portrayed in television and film as a vicious guard dog; two memorable Dobermans named Zeus and Apollo often appeared on the television show *Magnum P.I.*

GIANT SCHNAUZER
Working

The largest of the three Schnauzer breeds is the Giant Schnauzer, classified as a working dog. The others—the Standard Schnauzer and the Miniature Schnauzer—are terriers.

This dog comes from Germany, a result of crossing the Standard Schnauzer with sheepdogs of Germany and the black Great Dane. The Giant Schnauzer was originally a herding dog. He closely resembles the Briard and the Bouvier des Flandres. The fur of this breed is hard, wiry, and close to the body, and it is colored salt and pepper, pure black, or black and tan. He stands between twenty-three and twenty-seven inches high.

Being a robust and sinewy breed, the Giant Schnauzer is powerful in build, sound in both body and mind. This is another dog that has proved his adaptability to work as a police dog. He is exceedingly trainable, having a high-spirited temperament combined with reliability.

Riesenschnauze is the German name for the Giant Schnauzer.

Originally cattle-driving dogs in Bavaria, Giant Schnauzers are used today as police and military guard dogs.

According to *The Great Book of Dogs*, "during the second World War, so many Giant Schnauzers died at the side of German soldiers that the breed almost became extinct."

In nineteenth-century Germany, Giant Schnauzers were the mascots and guardians of butcher shops and beer halls.

GREAT DANE

FAWN VARIETY

Working

Though probably one of the oldest breeds in dogdom, the Great Dane owes his current beauty to development by German breeders who used the blood of the Irish Wolfhound and the Mastiff some four hundred years ago to obtain his litheness.

The Great Dane's first use was for boar hunting. This required a super dog because the wild boar was and still is one of the most savage, swift, and powerful of big game. Though he is an exceedingly capable dog, the Great Dane is also very affectionate and loyal.

This dog of such tremendous size—not under twenty-eight inches in height and weighing 120 to 160 pounds—is slow to act but never does anything illogically. He will never go out of his way to make trouble, but woe be to that dog or intruder who chooses to anger the Dane. In spite of his size, the Great Dane is gentle and handles himself well in the home.

The name Great Dane originated from the French term *Grand Danois*, meaning "big Dane."

Hanna-Barbera's animated Scooby-Doo and Astro (*The Jetsons*) and Brad Anderson's newspaper comic-strip character Marmaduke are all Great Danes.

Elvis Presley owned two Great Danes, which were named Snoopy and Brutus. Brutus appeared as Albert in the 1968 movie *Live a Little, Love a Little*.

A portrait of William Penn's Great Dane hangs in the governor's reception room in Harrisburg, Pennsylvania.

The Great Dane is the official state dog of Pennsylvania and the national dog of Germany.

President Franklin D. Roosevelt owned a Great Dane named President.

GREAT DANE
HARLEQUIN VARIETY
Working

The Great Dane, often called the King of Dogs, has a very short, thick, and glossy coat. There are five color varieties: brindle, fawn, blue, black, and harlequin. Fawn and harlequin are most frequently seen. The base color of the harlequin is white, with black spots irregularly and well distributed over the body.

There were probably Great Danes before the birth of Christ, but they are officially termed a German breed, their name being *Deutsche Dogge*.

There is no other breed that is more regal and stately-looking. Called the tallest of all dogs, he is nevertheless one of the most active and agile. He is a very dependable dog, a loving companion, and a worker capable of performing many services for humans. He has a good nose and can follow a trail accurately. He makes an effective dog for police work and can perform many other useful acts.

"Things that upset a Terrier may pass virtually unnoticed by a Great Dane."
—Smiley Blanton

Jacqueline Kennedy Onassis was famously photographed as a child with her family pet, a Great Dane named King Phar.

Andy Warhol owned a taxidermy Great Dane named Cecil, rumored to have been named after its former owner, Cecil B. DeMille. The dog stood guard at the entrance to Warhol's Factory, appeared in many of the artist's portraits, and now resides in the Andy Warhol Museum in Pittsburgh.

"The Great Dane had its period of greatest popularity in the 19th century in England when a horse and carriage was not considered complete unless it was preceded by at least two Harlequin Mastiffs."
—*The Great Book of Dogs*

GREAT PYRENEES
Working

The Great Pyrenees is also known as the Great Dog of the Mountains. He suggests a snow-white St. Bernard to the average observer. He is a very large dog, weighing up to 125 pounds and standing from twenty-five to thirty-two inches high.

The Great Pyrenees is a French breed. He has an ambling gait and is a beautiful, majestic dog to see. This breed is a strenuous worker. This has been proven by his ability to perform those duties for which he is famous—guarding flocks of sheep on the mountain slopes of the Pyrenees and serving as a draft dog.

This dog is both serious in his work and serious in his play. He is thoroughly devoted to humans, gentle, and even-tempered.

The elegant Great Pyrenees is ancient, having been depicted in Roman works of art thousands of years old.

This breed is called *Le Grand Chien des Montagnes* or *Le Chien des Pyrénées*, and the Pyrenees Mountain Dog.

Originally a dog of the peasantry, the Great Pyrenees became a dog of the French nobility in the seventeenth century, when the breed fell into the favor of the court of Louis XIV.

In 1824, French General Lafayette brought the first pair of Great Pyrenees to the United States.

This breed is believed to have originated in Central Asia or Siberia.

Inspired by the Great Pyrenees, renowned designer Javier Mariscal designed the 1992 Summer Olympic Games mascot, Cobi.

KOMONDOR
Working

Like the Puli and the Kuvasz, the Komondor is a Hungarian breed and is used extensively in that country as a sheepherder. He is a hardy dog of the outdoors and a trustworthy and capable dog for guarding both the home and the flock that may be entrusted to him.

The Komondor is similar to the Old English Sheep Dog, having a very long and shaggy coat that is only white in color. His height varies between twenty-two and twenty-six inches.

This woolly-looking dog possesses great endurance, the ability to stand guard over sheep in a herd for days at a time without help from man. His profuse coat gives him excellent protection from the worst weather. His heavy body gives him both power and the ability to be aggressive when the need arises. Although he is gentle in nature and easygoing under normal conditions, he can fight fiercely when he is challenged.

The Komondor is a descendant of Tibetan dogs and was brought to Hungary to guard flocks of sheep thousands of years ago by nomadic Magyars.

This dog's dreadlocked coat resembles a very large mop.

A Komondor jumping a hurdle is featured on the cover of Beck's 1996 album, *Odelay*.

The Komondor's coat is true white, but this is seen only at dog shows after several baths and intense grooming; otherwise, he is almost always gray.

"Komondork" is the plural form of "Komondor."

KUVASZ
Working

The Kuvasz is also known as the Hungarian Sheepdog and the dog of Hungarian royalty, having been a great favorite of past kings of the country. The name Kuvasz means "an armed guard for an ambassador or a nobleman."

Though this breed undoubtedly originated in Tibet, Hungarian breeders perfected the Kuvasz to develop his present-day value in herding. He is very active in movement and surprisingly light-footed for his size.

The Kuvasz is all white in color. The coat is slightly wavy and long. The height of this serious worker averages about twenty-eight inches, and he usually weighs between eighty and one hundred pounds.

This breed, though originally a guard dog for estates, where he proved to be very valuable during times of conflict, is also an excellent sheepherder, like his countryman the Komondor. He is one of the better breeds of large dogs used for this valuable service to humans.

In Turkish, *kuvasz* means "protector."

According to the American Kennel Club, "the Kuvasz's name comes from the corrupted spelling of the Turkish word *kawasz* (armed guard of nobility) and the Arabian word *kawwasz* (archer) that signified the unexcelled guarding instincts of the breed."

During the fifteenth century, King Matthias I was so enamored of his Kuvaszok, it was said that he trusted his dogs more than people.

In order to establish a deep connection with the flocks they protect, working Kuvasz puppies are brought up alongside the lambs. These fluffy white animals form a real friendship in which the sheep trust the dogs and the dogs feel responsible for the sheep.

MASTIFF
Working

Though an English breed, the Mastiff is much older, having originated in Egypt around 3000 B.C. The word *mastiff* comes from Latin and means "massive."

The Mastiff most assuredly is massive. He is among the most powerful of all breeds and, as authorities have said, is a "combination of grandeur and good nature, courage, and docility."

The Mastiff has a short coat lying close to his body. He is colored apricot, silver fawn, or a dark fawn brindle. The muzzle, ears, and nose are black. This dog can weigh more than two hundred pounds and stands about thirty inches in height.

Through the ages, the Mastiff has always been a guard dog of large estates. He is one of the most knowing dogs and is ever faithful to his duties toward humans.

This breed is also popularly known as Old English Mastiff, having been bred in England for more than two thousand years.

During Roman times, Mastiffs fought against human gladiators as well as bears, bulls, lions, and tigers in a bloody spectator sport.

Mastiffs were commonly used as war dogs. Kublai Khan is believed to have had a kennel of five thousand that he used in war and hunting.

According to *The Guinness Book of World Records*, the heaviest dog on record is an English Mastiff named Zorba, who weighs an astonishing 343 pounds.

Henry VIII is said to have given four hundred Mastiffs as a gift to Charles V of Spain.

It is believed that a Mastiff came to the United States from England on the *Mayflower*.

NEWFOUNDLAND
Working

The famed Newfoundlands have a reputation as savers of human lives that surpasses every other breed, except possibly the St. Bernard. Like the St. Bernard, the Newfoundland has rescued many people lost in snowstorms, but he is best known as a dog who has saved thousands of humans from drowning. The Newfoundland is at home in the water and can swim through currents of the ocean that humans could not withstand.

This heroic dog is large, weighing between 110 and 150 pounds and measuring about twenty-seven inches high at the shoulders. His heavy, dense coat enables him to withstand the iciest water and subzero weather for hours. He is usually all black but may be any solid color. There is also a strain named Landseer Newfoundland that is black and white.

The Newfoundland is very docile and gentle for his size. A true working type, he is good at herding and other general farm work.

In the famous children's classic *Peter Pan*, by J.M. Barrie, the Darling family pet is a Newfoundland named Nana.

This breed is nicknamed The Gentle Giant and Nature's Babysitter.

Famed fashion photographer Bruce Weber is also known for portraits of his larger-than-life Newfoundlands. These trademark dogs are not only featured in his fashion and advertising photographs but also are the stars of his book *Gentle Giant,* and movie *A Letter to True.*

A Newfoundland named Seaman accompanied his owners Lewis and Clark on their great expedition and is believed to have been responsible for saving their lives on many occasions. A commemorative statue of the explorers and their pet stands in Kansas City, Missouri.

"You ask of my Companion Hills – Sir – and the Sundown – and a Dog – large as myself."
—Emily Dickinson of her Newfoundland, Carlo, in a letter to Thomas Wentworth Higginson

ROTTWEILER
Working

The Rottweiler reflects outstanding solidity, is squarely built, and is among the most powerful of all breeds. He is a Roman dog, though he owes his development to German breeders who have used him for centuries in draft work and as a farm dog. The German police have found the dignified Rottweiler useful for certain types of work, and there are many of these dogs used on the police force there.

The Rottweiler is another member of the black and tan family, being colored black with tan markings, the same as the Doberman Pinscher. He stands between twenty-two and twenty-seven inches in height.

This courageous dog seldom permits anything to excite him. He moves easily, without hesitation, and has no fear. He is naturally obedient and this, plus his natural desire to please, makes him a dog that is very easily trained for various types of useful work.

"About 700 A.D., the local Duke of Arae Flaviae (what is now southern Germany) ordered a Christian church built on the site of the former Roman baths. Excavations unearthed the red tiles of Roman villas; to distinguish the town, it was then named *Das Rote Wil*, "the red tile," which is of course recognizable as the derivation of the present Rottweiler."

—The American Kennel Club

In Germany, the Rottweiler was called the *Rottweil Metzgerhund*, meaning "butcher dog," as the breed hauled carts for butchers and cattle dealers.

Alexandra Day's children's book series *Good Dog, Carl* features a lovable Rottweiler.

In the 1980s classic film *Ferris Bueller's Day Off*, the Buellers' ferocious family pet is a Rottweiler.

ST. BERNARD
Working

Though the St. Bernard, as seen today, is a dog with a long coat, our forefathers knew him to be a short-coated breed. It is this later type that has been glorified as the saver of human lives in the Swiss mountain regions.

The St. Bernard's huge size is his greatest asset in this work. He is the heaviest of all dogs—some specimens weighing more than two hundred pounds. The height is around twenty-seven inches, not as high as that of the Great Dane and a few other breeds.

This fine dog needs no training. He is a natural guard and an ideal protector of children, having no trace of viciousness and being very even-tempered. His tremendous weight does not prevent the St. Bernard from being gentle in his movement. He is very sure of himself and is very dignified. Few other breeds possess the noble St. Bernard's deep philosophic quality of faithfulness and devotion.

These dogs served as guard dogs at hospices located in the Swiss Alps, and they were companions to the monks living there. Thanks to their dogs' impeccable sense of smell, these monks would locate and save lost and freezing travelers. According to the American Kennel Club, they "saved over 2,000 lives" in their three centuries of work.

While St. Bernards are often portrayed wearing a small brandy-filled barrel around their necks, the dogs never really carried alcohol. Sir Edwin Landseer's portrait of a St. Bernard rescuing a traveler supposedly inspired this myth; the artist added the casks of brandy as an amusing detail.

A St. Bernard named Chris played the naughty family dog in the *Beethoven* films.

Barry—the most famous St. Bernard—rescued between forty and one hundred people in the Alps. His body is preserved in the Natural History Museum in Berne, Switzerland, and there is a monument in his honor at the *Cimetière des Chiens*.

SAMOYED
Working

The Samoyed is essentially a worker, a valuable asset of the Samoyed people in the Siberian valley as both a sled dog and a herding dog of endurance.

This is a beautiful dog, with his long coat of white, biscuit, or cream, his bushy tail carried over his back, his smiling face, and his grace in movement. He stands between eighteen and twenty-three inches at the shoulder and weighs from thirty-six to fifty-five pounds, the female of the breed being slightly smaller.

The Samoyed is a beauty in disposition, too. He has a marvelously even temperament, is always trustworthy, and is a splendid dog around children. He never makes trouble but is able to hold his own when forced into a fight.

This northern dog can withstand severe cold weather, and yet, due to a double coat that gives protection from the sun, he does not mind hot weather.

In 1911, Samoyeds accompanied Roald Amundsen in his landmark journey to the South Pole.

This breed is sometimes called the Smiley Dog, Smiley Sammy, or Happy Sammy because of its joyful facial expression.

It is believed that in Siberia, Samoyed dogs slept with their owners to keep them warm at night.

Some knitters use Samoyed fur as an alternative to wool.

Queen Alexandra of England was an admirer of the Samoyed breed.

The Samoyed is often called the *Bjelkier* in Europe.

SIBERIAN HUSKY
Working

This capable sled puller of the Arctic regions, particularly northeastern Siberia, is an affectionate dog, although he will not make friends with strangers. It might be said that humans cannot make friends with him; he must take the initiative if any friendship is to be formed.

The Siberian Husky is an exceptionally active dog with the power to pull heavy sleds over long distances. He has a rugged, strong body covered with a thick, furry coat that may be colored from black to gray or have mixed wolf markings. The breed is about twenty-two inches high and weighs from forty-four to fifty-five pounds.

His prowess at pulling sleds in harness has won him many honors in sled racing, as he is able to run at a speed as high as twenty miles an hour over surprisingly long distances.

The Siberian Husky is known to be a great pet for children. He loves to be around them and will play with them tirelessly for several hours at a time.

The Cheukchi tribe of northeastern Asia developed Siberian Huskies as sled dogs, as they needed dogs with the ability to travel long distances while carrying light loads in subzero temperatures.

Although his lineage remains uncertain, Balto is perhaps the most famous Siberian Husky of all time. In 1925, he led a team of Huskies 650 miles across Alaska, transporting a diphtheria serum through a blizzard. Today, the Iditarod Sled Race annually commemorates this historic event. A statue of Balto stands in New York City's Central Park.

In the show ring, Siberian Huskies are one of the few breeds for which there is no set standard for eye color. Eyes can be blue, hazel, or brown, but light blue is the most common. One unique acceptable trait: When one eye is colored blue and the other colored brown or hazel, this is known as being bi-eyed.

Huskies were the stars of the Disney movies *Snow Dogs* and *Eight Below*.

BELGIAN SHEEPDOG
Herding

World War I brought the Belgian Sheepdog into prominence as a messenger on the front lines. This dog is often confused with the German Shepherd Dog; however, he is smaller and less stocky, standing about twenty-two to twenty-six inches in height and weighing a little more than fifty pounds.

Two other types of work mark the Belgian Sheepdog—one, a police dog, and the other, a herding dog. The little country of Belgium is characterized by frequent weather changes, and this breed was perfected to withstand almost any weather while guarding its flocks.

The Belgian Sheepdog possesses the uncanny quality of always being able to discern and adjust himself to the moods of his master.

Originally, the black Belgian Sheepdog was to be named after his developer, Monsieur Rose, but later it was determined that Rose was not an appropriate name for a black dog. Instead, the name Groenendael was chosen, after Monsieur Rose's castle.

Today, there are four known varieties of the Belgian Sheepdog. The Groenendael, the most popular, has a black, long-haired coat; the Laekenois has a fawn, rough coat; the Malinois has a short fawn-and-mahogany coat with black marks and overlay; and the Tervuren has a fawn, mahogany, or gray long coat with black mask and overlay. The American Kennel Club recognizes these varieties, with the exception of the Laekenois.

A Tervuren Belgian Sheepdog named Kyte plays Wellard, the canine star of the popular BBC soap opera *EastEnders*.

BOUVIER DES FLANDRES
Herding

The Bouvier des Flandres is a herding dog of Belgium. He is also often used for guarding, police work, and as a defense dog.

This breed resembles the Giant Schnauzer to some extent, standing from twenty-three to twenty-eight inches high. The coat is rough in texture and is colored fawn, pepper, gray, or black. Some white on the chest is permissible.

The general appearance of the Bouvier des Flandres is that of a vigorous, rugged working type. He is powerfully built, though not particularly heavy for his height. His body is compact, and the harsh coat enables him to withstand strenuous work in almost any weather.

This is another breed that was used extensively during World War I as a messenger and for accompanying ambulances.

The Bouvier des Flandres is one of the rarer breeds in North America.

The French word *bouvier* means "cowherd" or "ox driver."

This breed is also known as the *Vuilbaard* ("dirty beard"), *Koehond* ("cow dog"), and *Toucheur de Boeuf* ("cattle driver").

President Ronald Reagan had a Bouvier named Lucky who literally tried to herd the president and his wife on many occasions, resulting in several embarrassing photo-ops. Because of her constant herding antics, Lucky was sent off to live at the Reagans' private ranch in California.

The American Kennel Club says that "in Belgium, a Bouvier cannot win the title of champion unless he has also won a prize in work competition as a police, defense, or army dog."

After World War I, the town of Flandres was completely destroyed, and the Bouvier breed was close to extinction. However, the breed was revived and a club was established to ensure its longevity.

BRIARD

Herding

The Briard, or *Chien Berger de Brie*, is a substantially built dog and one of the few originating in France. He is many centuries old. The Briard has outstanding ability as a herding dog, though he is also used extensively for draft work and as a watchdog. He is strictly an outdoor dog, powerfully built, well proportioned, and active.

The long coat of the Briard falls over the eyes, similarly to that of the Old English Sheepdog. The coat can be any solid dark color, white being absolutely outlawed, but some combination of colors is allowed.

The height of this squarely built breed is between twenty-two and twenty-eight inches at the shoulders.

Briards are rather slow to train, but once a duty or trick is learned, it is never forgotten. They thoroughly enjoy their work and do best when given the opportunity to use their own initiative, which makes them another breed very useful for war and police duties.

Charlemagne bred some of the first Briards in France, which led the breed to become the country's most popular sheepdog.

Thomas Jefferson and Marquis de Lafayette were both fond of Briards and are credited with bringing the breed to North America.

Tramp—the family pet in the classic 1960s television series *My Three Sons*—was a Briard.

During World War I, the Briards' acute sense of hearing helped them to alert soldiers in the French army of imminent danger. This breed also possesses an astonishing instinct for locating the wounded and identifying those who are most severely hurt and in need of immediate medical attention.

This extremely old French breed has been depicted in tapestries dating back as early as the eighth century.

COLLIE
Herding

The Collie came into popularity as a result of his being a superior herding dog in the hills of Scotland; however, it is generally believed that the Collie is a much more ancient breed. Years ago, this dog was strictly a working dog of hardy character. Today, though he retains his strong qualities, the Collie is a picture of grace and agility. This was possibly accomplished through a breeding cross with the Borzoi.

This famous dog, with his abundant coat, can withstand the severest weather. He is clearly a working dog, combining beauty and the ability to drive cattle for many hours. There are three types of Collie—the rough and the smooth, which are the same except for the coat, and the Shetland Sheepdog, a separately recognized breed, a Collie in miniature. The smooth Collie is known to be a drover's dog, guiding sheep and cattle, while the rough variety guards the herd in the pasture.

The name Collie probably comes from its charge—the Scottish black-faced sheep called the Colley.

Albert Payson Terhune's 1919 story *Lad: A Dog* has been read by several generations of Americans. Collie fanciers gather each year at Sunnybrooke Farm at Lake Pompton, New Jersey, to pay tribute to Lad on his birthday and to raise money to support the breed's health research.

The most famous Collie was Lassie. The original Lassie, "Pal," was a rescue dog. He was unwanted by his owners and given to the trainer Rudd Weatherwax. Pal auditioned twice for the role of Lassie and was turned down. After Pal gave a brilliant performance while filling in for a show Collie that refused to go into the water, the director said, "Pal may have gone into the water, but it was Lassie that came out."

Elvis Presley owned a Collie named Baba, which appeared with him in the 1966 film *Paradise, Hawaiian Style*.

GERMAN SHEPHERD DOG
Herding

This breed is frequently referred to as the German Police Dog due to his wide use in this work. The German Shepherd Dog is highly adaptable to training, and many are trained as seeing-eye dogs for the blind, guard dogs, and protectors. World War I found this dog also used extensively as a messenger and ambulance dog in the frontline trenches.

The German Shepherd is known as the king of dogs. The breed is large enough to tackle humans yet agile enough to cope with a flock of sheep. The breed possesses a character combining loyalty and honesty in addition to an ability to assimilate and retain training for many different services to mankind. He is an intelligent dog with the power to judge for himself. He is dignified and, though rather suspicious of strangers, is a real friend to his home and family.

The coat is rather dense, straight, and of medium length. Colors of the breed vary from white to black, and most dogs are a wolfish-gray color.

The German Shepherd has more than 225 million cell receptors in its nose, making it ideal for police work. The K-9 Corps—including the Army, Navy, Marines, and Coast Guard—use the German Shepherd for his bravery, intelligence, and steadfastness.

The German Shepherd Rin Tin Tin was one of the most famous canine movie stars of all time. He starred in twenty-four films and is credited with saving Warner Brothers from bankruptcy.

In order to avoid affiliation with Germany during World War I and World War ll, this breed was renamed the Alsatian. The name was changed back to the German Shepherd in 1977.

In the aftermath of the terrorist attacks on September 11, 2001, German Shepherds were part of a group of more than three hundred dogs used in the search-and-rescue operation.

OLD ENGLISH SHEEPDOG

Herding

With his very shaggy coat completely hiding his head and eyes, the Old English Sheepdog looks more like a moving pile of fuzzy wool than like a competent working dog. He is truly a picturesque dog, with his profuse coat and beautiful slow, ambling gait.

Though named Old English Sheepdog, this bearlike canine is really a dog for cattle, and it is probable that the Russian Sheepdog was his predominating ancestor, along with the old bearded Collies. Due to his coat, this breed looks much larger than he actually is. He stands between twenty-one and twenty-two inches high.

The Old English Sheepdog is never ferocious or boisterous. He is a fine, all-purpose working dog, for his great intelligence makes him a good retriever and a smart rabbit hunter as well as a good herder, his better-known ability. He is a tireless dog, always full of energy and more steady and sure in his movements than quick.

Martha was an Old English Sheepdog who belonged to Paul McCartney and was the subject of the song "Martha My Dear" on the Beatles' *White Album*.

The Old English Sheepdog has been featured in films such as *The Shaggy Dog* series and *Please Don't Eat the Daisies*.

It is said that in the eighteenth century, the Old English Sheepdog's tail was docked in order to identify tax-exempt herding dogs, giving them their nickname Bobtail.

President Franklin D. Roosevelt owned an Old English Sheepdog named Tiny.

The Old English Sheepdog has a distinguishing gait that is similar to the movement of a bear.

PULI
Herding

This medium-size dog used as a herder of sheep in the Hungarian hills is accustomed to one master and is quite suspicious of strangers. The Puli is an extremely active dog and could be called an Old English Sheep Dog of small stature were it not for his rapidity of movement.

His coat is very long and profuse, especially on the head and face. The hair may be perfectly straight, wavy, or curly and of any color. Due to his long coat, the Puli appears to be a much larger dog than he actually is. He stands from sixteen to seventeen inches high.

This alert herding dog is a serviceable type and has been relied upon to guard sheep for his master for many years. He is intelligent and trustworthy and possesses the courage to stand up for his rights whether he is in his home surroundings or in a strange place.

Ancestors of the Puli were introduced in Hungary in the Middle Ages, when the Magyars migrated from Central Asia.

The Puli's corded coat is similar to that of the Komondor. These tight curls make the breed's fur virtually waterproof.

"Pulik" is the plural form of "Puli."

Singers Gavin Rossdale and Gwen Stefani had a Puli named Winston.

Tallulah Bankhead had a Puli called Donnie, which was named after Donald Cook, her co-star in Noel Coward's play *Private Lives*.

SHETLAND SHEEPDOG
Herding

Though the Shetland Sheepdog is classified as the ideal Collie in miniature, this excellent sheep hunter is far from small in usefulness, for he has been a capable herder for many years, chasing adventurous sheep over the mountainous hills of the Shetland Islands.

The Shetland Sheepdog is a typical small Collie, standing, on average, fourteen inches tall. Were it not for the difference in size, the two could hardly be distinguished.

This fine-dispositioned breed is among the most obedient of all dogs. Shelties, as they are often called, are intelligent and ever desirous of pleasing their owners. This characteristic shows in their happy and interesting facial expressions.

Contrary to what one might think when considering the small size of the Shetland Sheepdog, he is capable of good, hard work over a period of many hours without tiring to any great degree.

The animals that reside on the Shetland Islands are smaller than those found on the mainland, which is why breeders developed a smaller Collie—the Shetland Sheepdog—to tend to the smaller-scale sheep.

"Unlike many other breeds, the Sheltie tends to be a 'one person' rather than a 'one family' dog. Although devoted to the entire family, it will single out its favorite member."
—*Dogs*

President Calvin Coolidge owned a Shetland Sheepdog named Calamity Jane.

At the end of the classic Beatles song "A Day in the Life," Paul McCartney recorded a whistle audible only to dogs in honor of his Shetland Sheedog.

WELSH CORGI
CARDIGAN VARIETY
Herding

The two Welsh Corgis—Cardigan and Pembroke, which are separate breeds—have a distinct duty to perform in their native country of Wales. Whereas the Collie herds cattle in the pasture and brings them home in the evening, the Welsh Corgi drives them out to pasture in the early hours of the morning. He runs between the herd, nipping at their heels until they are out in the field so the Collie can take over the work.

The Welsh Corgi's herding value is not confined to cattle alone. He herds all kinds of farm stock, including pigs, and is a fine all-around dog for the farm.

The two breeds of Welsh Corgi may be any color, with coats of medium length. The principal difference is their tails—the Cardigan has a long, natural tail, and the Pembroke, a docked, or cut, tail.

The name Corgi is derived from the Welsh words *cor* meaning "dwarf" and *gi* meaning "dog."

The Cardigan Welsh Corgi is the older of the two Corgi breeds and is believed to be one of the oldest of all dog breeds.

In the 1988 film *The Accidental Tourist*, a Cardigan Welsh Corgi stars alongside Geena Davis, who plays his trainer.

The Cardigan Welsh Corgi is a descendant of the Teckel (Dachshund) family and is therefore said to be a distant relative of the Dachshund.

The Cardigan Welsh Corgi was introduced to Wales by the Celts.

WELSH CORGI
PEMBROKE VARIETY
Herding

Welsh Corgis are among the most agreeable dogs. They make good house dogs in addition to being valuable farm guards and herders of livestock. Few breeds equal the Corgi's desire to please, and yet they do not force their attentions on those who do not desire them.

The Welsh Corgi breeds, Cardigan and Pembroke, are big little dogs. Hardy in construction and capable of performing many duties on the farm, they have been great aids to Welshmen since the year 1107.

The Pembroke is a trifle higher than the Cardigan, standing under twelve inches, and less lengthy in body. Besides the difference in tails mentioned in the section on the Cardigan Welsh Corgi, the Pembroke has pointed ears as compared with the rounded ears of the Cardigan. Other than the differences in size, length of tail, and ears, these two distinct breeds are similar. Both possess remarkably useful intelligence and are ever loyal to their masters.

In 1107, Flemish weavers brought Pemboke Welsh Corgis to Wales to use as cattle dogs.

The Pembroke Welsh Corgi is a favorite of Queen Elizabeth II, and she is frequently photographed with them in tow. Most of these dogs are descendants of Susan, a Corgi that the Queen received for her eighteenth birthday.

The word *corgi* is also used to mean "rascal" in the south of Wales.

The Pembroke Welsh Corgi is the younger and more popular of the two Corgi breeds.

BOSTON TERRIER
Non-Sporting

Brindle Bull, Boston Bulldog, Boston Bullterrier—these are some of the names often erroneously given to the North American–originated Boston Terrier. This breed was created around the middle of the nineteenth century from two other breeds of the bulldog type, the English Terrier and the Bulldog, and it is one of the few North American dogs.

The expression of the Boston Terrier indicates a high degree of intelligence.

In appearance, the Boston is distinctive. He is small and short-haired, making him an ideal house dog. He has a genial disposition and has little use for fighting, being too filled up with play to give fighting much thought. However, this same liveliness makes him an alert, barking watchdog for the home. Life is seldom dull for the Boston.

The breed has three weight classes for show purposes, the lightweight less than fifteen pounds; middleweight, fifteen to twenty pounds; heavyweight, twenty to twenty-five pounds.

Due to his gentle character and pleasant disposition, this breed was often called the American Gentleman in the nineteenth century.

In 1979, the Boston Terrier was recognized by the Massachusetts state legislature as the official state dog.

In the *Oz* book series, the character of Toto was drawn as a Boston Terrier instead of a Cairn Terrier, which ultimately earned the role in the movie.

The Boston Terrier is frequently featured in advertising, such as Badger, the lost dog in many MasterCard television commercials.

A Boston Terrier named Rhett is the mascot for Boston University.

BULLDOG
Non-Sporting

The Bulldog from England's is one of the more grouchy-looking breeds, yet he is one of the gentlest. This dog, often termed The Sour Mug, is England's national dog. His name comes from his original use, bull baiting, which was once a popular sport in Great Britain.

The Bulldog makes a great companion for a child, who may do practically anything to him, and he still retains his good nature.

The powerful chest and general sturdiness of the Bulldog show him to be a breed with great endurance and stability. He is dignified in everything he does. He is easygoing and seldom allows another dog to excite him, though he is courageous and well able to care for himself when the need arises.

Bulldogs weigh between forty and fifty pounds. Their weight is shown in bulkiness rather than in height, for they are quite short-legged. Their short, dense coat is colored uniformly over the body.

"Do you know why the English Bulldog has a jutting chin and a sloping face? It is so he can breathe without letting go."
—Sir Winston Churchill, who was famously nicknamed the Bulldog due to his similar facial features and character

Comedian Adam Sandler's English Bulldog—Meatball—was best man at his wedding and wore a tuxedo and yarmulke. Sandler has since acquired another Bulldog, Matzoball.

The Bulldog is the most popular canine mascot for North American schools and universities, including Yale's Handsome Dan and Georgetown University's Jack the Bulldog.

President Warren Harding owned a Bulldog named Oh Boy, and President Calvin Coolidge had one named Boston Beans.

The Bulldog is both the logo and the medallion for Mack Truck, one of the world's leading truck companies.

CHOW CHOW
Non-Sporting

Of the three breeds from China—Chow Chow, Pekingese, and Pug—the Chow is the most Asian in appearance. Though classed as a non-sporting breed, these dogs have been bred by the Chinese for centuries as herding, sledge, and hunting dogs.

The Chow is the only breed of dog that has a blue-black tongue. This shows that he is not closely related to any other breed. The coat is a massive fluff of fur of any solid color. The head, with its scowling face, is very similar to that of a lion.

The Chow's personality is distinctive. No other breed is so proud, so aloof. He has little to do with strangers and is very loyal to his home and master; being a very patient dog, he is a great companion for children.

Due to his bluish tongue and ancient lineage, there is some cause to believe that the Chow is one of the basic breeds of dogdom from which many of today's breeds came.

In China, this breed is referred to as the *Songshi Quan*, meaning "puffy, lion dog." It has also been called the *Tang Quan*, "dog of the Tang Empire."

The name of this breed originates from the Chinese word *Chaou*, meaning "large, primitive, undomesticated, extraordinary dog of great strength." It is also believed to have evolved from a Pidgin English slang term for eighteenth-century Asian knickknacks.

Han Dynasty statues of Chow Chow dogs were discovered in noblemen's graves; it was believed that the statues guarded their masters from evil spirits.

President Calvin Coolidge had a Chow named Timmy; Sigmund Freud owned two, Jofi and Lunyu; Elvis Presley owned one named Getio; and Martha Stewart has owned many, including Paw-Paw, Chin Chin, Zu-Zu, and Empress Wu.

DALMATIAN
Non-Sporting

Dalmatians have been famous for years as a breed that loves to be around horses. They became known as the Coach Dog, and the Firehouse Dog. Prior to the automobile, Dalmatians were always found at the livery stables. The coat of the Dalmatian has given him still a third nickname, that of Plum Pudding Dog, derived from the markings on the coat—either black or liver spots on white.

This breed originated in the small Adriatic province of Dalmatia, which is now a part of Croatia. Some believe him to be the ancestor of the Pointer, which closely resembles him.

The Dalmatian is an all-around dog. He is a great companion, never noisy, aggressive, or vicious; he is adaptable to many purposes. The Dalmatian is a medium-size dog, weighing thirty-five to fifty pounds and standing from nineteen to twenty-two inches high.

Dalmatian puppies are born white; their spots appear gradually as they grow.

This breed grew in popularity as a result of Dodie Smith's 1956 novel *The Hundred and One Dalmatians*. Disney successfully released two films based on the book about the charming canine couple Pongo and Perdita, and their fifteen puppies, which—as the story goes—amazingly turn into 101 Dalmatians.

".... the Dalmatian is distinguished by the fact that he will follow his master constantly, whether he is on foot, on horseback, or riding a bicycle. In 1800, in fact, he was known as the 'Promenade Dog.'"
—*The Great Book of Dogs*

Historically, Dalmatians were used to guard the wagons of beer brewers while they made deliveries. Today, this tradition continues with the signature Dalmatian atop the Anheuser-Busch Company's iconic beer wagon, famously pulled by a team of magnificent Clydesdale horses.

FRENCH BULLDOG
Non-Sporting

French Bulldogs, though originating probably in France, owe their advancement to English dog fanciers who have been breeding them since the middle of the nineteenth century.

The French Bulldog stands out for his batlike ears, quizzical expression, and rather rolling gait. He is clownish when he wants to be but also can be very dignified. These characteristics make him a good playmate for a child and an excellent house dog. His size, plus his personality, show him to be a breed easily adapted to living in confined quarters.

There are two weight classes for the French Bulldog; lightweights are under twenty-two pounds, while heavyweights are between twenty-two and twenty-eight pounds.

The coat is short, fine, and of brilliant texture. The color can be brindle, fawn, white, or brindle and white. Pure black is a disqualifying color.

This breed is gentle, clean, and always dependable.

The French Bulldog's original name was the *Boule Chien Français* or *Bouledogue*.

In the late 1800s, this dog was extremely popular with fashion-savvy French women and was often seen adorned with an elaborate feathered collar.

Martha Stewart appeared on the cover of *Vanity Fair* magazine with her black French Bulldog, Francesca. She has another French Bulldog named Sharky.

"It remains an established fact, however, that around the middle of the 19th century, the French Bulldog virtually invaded Paris, especially in the working class districts where there was hardly a coachman or butcher who did not own one."
—*The Great Book of Dogs*

Actor Nathan Lane owns a French Bulldog named Mabel.

KEESHOND
Non-Sporting

The Keeshond ("Keeshonden" is the plural form of the name) is a cheerful dog, a contented dog. He is a delightful companion, happy anywhere, and can live either in the house or outdoors. He is of good medium size, standing around sixteen inches in height, and is very hardy.

This dog is the national dog of Holland and has been known as Holland's barge dog for centuries, though in all probability, he originated in the Arctic regions along with the Samoyed, the Chow, and others of northern breeding. His coat is full and heavy, colored a silver-gray with black-tipped fur and with lighter shades on the head, legs, stomach, and tail. His face is a dark mask.

The Keeshond is called an ideal companion dog. He is a good watchdog, being rather distrustful of strangers and ever faithful to his home and to those duties given to him to perform. Keeshonden possess a real canine personality.

This dog is also known as the Dutch Barge Dog, as it was commonly used to guard barges traveling the Rhine River.

The Keeshond was the mascot of the Patriot Party in eighteenth-century Holland. The breed takes his name from the party's leader, Cornelis "Kees" de Gyselaer, who led the rebellion against William V of Orange.

Thanks to a sunny disposition, this breed is sometimes called the Smiling Dutchman.

The Keeshond is a descendant of the Finnish Spitz breed.

POODLE
Non-Sporting

Classed as a non-sporting breed, the Poodle was once one of the best of hunting dogs and an unexcelled water retriever. Due to his remarkable aptitude for learning tricks, he has become better known as a stage dog. His very appearance strongly suggests intelligence and pride.

There are three varieties of the Poodle, though only two distinctly recognized breeds—the Toy Poodle and the Poodle. The last is divided into Miniature and Standard varieties. Standards stand more than fifteen inches high, while Miniatures are under that height. All three may have coats either curly or corded. They may be any solid or even color, though whites and blacks are most frequently seen.

The Poodle is a stylish-looking dog and attracts attention wherever he may be. He is an ideal show dog. The manner in which his naturally profuse coat is clipped gives him a clownish appearance but, at the same time, a smart and elegant one as well.

This breed's name is derived from the German word *Pudel* or *Pudelhund*, from the Old German word *Puddeln*, meaning "to splash it out." In France, the Poodle is known as the *Caniche*.

John Steinbeck's Poodle, Charlie, was the inspiration for his book *Travels with Charlie*.

"Poodles always listen attentively while being scolded, looking innocent, bewildered, and misunderstood."
—James Thurber

The richest dog in the world is said to be a Poodle named Toby, who inherited $75 million from his owner, millionaire Ella Wendal.

Miss Piggy, the melodramatic star of *The Muppet Show*, has a Poodle named Foo-Foo.

President Richard Nixon owned a Poodle named Vicky, and Winston Churchill owned one named Rufus.

SCHIPPERKE
Non-Sporting

Inquisitive, indefatigable, affectionate—these words best describe the little Schipperke from Holland and Belgium. He is used as a barge dog in the low countries, his very name meaning "little captain."

The Schipperke is never without curiosity, always wondering what is going on behind closed doors. This quality, and his suspiciousness, makes him a fine watchdog, one who gives immediate warning of any intrusion to his domicile with a shrill bark. He is a useful breed in other ways, too, being a good killer of vermin and a faithful guardian of children.

The coat of the Schipperke is always pure black, somewhat harsh to the touch and abundant, especially about the neck, chest, and over the rear of his hind legs. There are three sizes of Schipperkes known, weighing between six and a half to eighteen pounds.

The Schipperke tends to be a one-person dog, preferring to lavish his affections on one owner rather than on an entire family.

"There is a story that two centuries ago, there was a cobbler who was envious of the Schipperke belonging to one of his colleagues; so, with his leather knife, he cut off the dog's tail. Surprisingly, the mutilation aroused enthusiasm instead of horror and the Association of Schipperke breeders decreed that the tales of all welps should be docked."
—*The Great Book of Dogs*

This dog is often called the Little Skipper or the Little Captain in honor of Captain Renssens, who developed the breed.

This breed is widely known as the Belgian Barge Dog, as it was recognized for its ability to rid barges and ships of vermin. Luckily, the Schipperke is not prone to seasickness.

THE MIXED BREED

The original edition of *The Blue Book of Dogs* did not include a section on mixed-breed dogs, probably because it is their pure bred relatives that take center stage in competition and the public eye. Nevertheless, these dogs—bred from any assortment of pure breeds or mutts—are just as adorable, loyal, and full of personality as their pedigree cousins.

Unfortunately, so many of these mixed-breed dogs are abandoned or given to animal shelters, but if they are lucky enough to find an owner, they too will become loyal companions and friends.

Recently, there has been a controversial trend in the dog world regarding the introduction of "dog hybrids" or "designer dogs" such as the Puggle (Pug-Beagle mix) and the Labradoodle (Labrador Retriever-Poodle mix). While the verdict is still out about the future of these deliberately mixed breeds, one thing is certain. Regardless of their ancestry or lack of pedigree, throughout history, the mixed-breed dog has always been an important member of the canine race, especially to those who have owned or loved one.

"I like a bit of a mongrel myself, whether it's a man or a dog; it's the best for every day."
—George Bernard Shaw

"Does the mixed breed compensate for lack of family background with intelligence superior to that of the purebred? Ask the man who owns one, but don't expect an unprejudiced answer."
—Morgan Dennis, painter of dogs

These beloved dogs are referred to as mongrels or mutts, originating from the word "muttonhead."

A mutt named Laika became the first living creature to orbit space in November 1957.

Sandy—the beloved pet of Little Orphan Annie—was a mixed-breed dog.

LIST OF BREEDS

Alaskan Malamute
American Water Spaniel
Belgian Sheepdog
Bernese Mountain Dog
Boston Terrier
Bouvier des Flandres
Boxer
Briard
Brittany Spaniel
Bulldog
Bullmastiff
Chesapeake Bay Retriever
Chow Chow
Clumber Spaniel
Cocker Spaniel, American
Cocker Spaniel, English
Collie
Curly-Coated Retriever
Dalmatian

Doberman Pinscher
English Setter
Field Spaniel
Flat-Coated Retriever
French Bulldog
German Shepherd Dog
German Shorthaired Pointer
Giant Schnauzer
Golden Retriever
Gordon Setter
Great Dane, Fawn
Great Dane, Harlequin
Great Pyrenees
Irish Setter
Irish Water Spaniel
Keeshond
Komondor
Kuvasz
Labrador Retriever

Mastiff
Newfoundland
Old English Sheepdog
Pointer
Poodle
Puli
Rottweiler
Samoyed
Schipperke
Shetland Sheepdog
Siberian Husky
Springer Spaniel, English
Springer Spaniel, Welsh
St. Bernard
Sussex Spaniel
Wirehaired Pointing Griffon
Welsh Corgi, Cardigan
Welsh Corgi, Pembroke

BIBLIOGRAPHY

Albin, Dickie, et al., *The Dog*. New York: Exeter Books, 1982.

The American Kennel Club. *The Complete Dog Book, 20th Edition.* New York: Ballantine Books, 2006.

Big Dogs, Little Dogs, the World of Our Canine Companions. A&E. New York: GT Publishing Corporation, 1998.

Boorer, Wendy, John Holmes, Margaret Osborne, Mary Roslin-Williams, Alan Hitchins, and Howard Loxton. *The Love of Dogs.* London: Octopus Books Ltd., 1974.

Cobb, Bert. *Hunting Dogs.* New York: The Crafton Collection, Inc., 1931.

———. *Portraits of Dogs.* New York: The Crafton Collection, Inc., 1931.

Cook, Gladys Emerson. *American Champions.* New York: The Macmillan Company, 1945.

Dawson, Lucy. *Dogs As I See Them.* New York: Grosset & Dunlap, 1937.

———. *Dogs Rough and Smooth.* New York: Grosset & Dunlap, 1936.

Dawson, Major A. J. *Everybody's Dog Book.* New York: Frederick A. Stokes Company, 1922.

———. *Everybody's Dog Book.* London: Philip Allan, 1933.

Dennis, Morgan. *The Morgan Dennis Dog Book (with Some Special Cats).* New York: The Viking Press, 1946.

Dudman, Helga. *The Dog's Guide to Famous Owners.* Great Britain: Robson Books Ltd., 1997.

Hutchinson, Walter, ed. *Hutchinson's Popular and Illustrated Dog Encyclopaedia.* London: Hutchinson & Co. Ltd., 1935.

Johnson, Thomas H., ed. *The Letters of Emily Dickinson.*
Cambridge, Mass., and London: The Belknap Press of Harvard
University Press, 1958.

Lawson, James Gilchrist. *The Book of Dogs.*
Chicago: Rand McNally & Company, 1934.

Mery, Ferdinand. *The Dog.*
London: Cassell & Company Ltd., 1968.

Pugnetti, Gino. *The Great Book of Dogs: An International
Anthology.* New York: Galahad Books, 1973.

Shuttlesworth, Dorothy. *The Story of Dogs.*
Garden City, N.Y.: Doubleday & Co., Inc., 1961.

Terhune, Albert Payson. *Real Tales of Real Dogs.*
Akron, Ohio: Saalfield Publishing Company, 1935.

Thorne, Diana. *Your Dogs and Mine.*
New York: Loring & Mussey, 1935.

WEB REFERENCES

akc.org
animatch.ca/en-dogfacts.htm
bird-dog-news.com
blurtit.com
bond.senate.org
britannica.com
british-manchester-terrier-
club.co.uk
celebritydogblog.com
chinpuppies.com
dogbreedinfo.com
dog-names.org
earlywomenmasters.net
eBay.com
edinburougharchitecture.co.uk
eisenhower.archives.gov
faqs.org
5stardog.com
filmsite.org

historyplace.com
hsus.org
irishfieldsports.com
litency.com
littlepaws.com
marilynfan.org
martycrisp.com
mdkidspage.org
nationalgeographic.com
olive-drab.com
pbs.org
petnet.com
petplanet.co.uk
puppydogweb.com
quoatations.about.com
thebreedsofdogs.com
titanic.com
wikipedia.com
wkc.org

And all of the individual dog-breed/club websites.

ACKNOWLEDGMENTS

I WOULD LIKE TO EXTEND A VERY SPECIAL THANK YOU TO THE FOLLOWING:

The American Kennel Club for the use of their archive collection, specifically Megan Lyons and Kira Sexton, for their help with collecting the many images from the archive.

My assistant and dear friend, **Daphne Birch**, for diligently helping to organize the insurmountable array of images and information in this book.

Art director and designer, **Ilana Anger** and Agnieszka Stachowicz, for elegantly capturing all the wonderful dogs in this book's bright and whimsical design.

Dinah Fried, the most efficient, hardworking, and pleasant editor one could ever have.

And senior editor, Elizabeth Viscott Sullivan, for her extraordinary love of dogs, especially Otis and Lulu, and her amazing ability to continue to raise the bar in her quest for excellence.